WIZARD MAGIC MAZES

by Roger Moreau

Sterling Publishing Co., Inc.
New York

Library of Congress Cataloging-in-Publication Data

Moreau, Roger, 1935-

   Wizard magic mazes/Roger Moreau.

      p. cm.

Includes index.

Summary: A collection of twenty-nine mazes which, together, lead the reader to Wizardry castle, where the Grand Wizard of Wigglewand's power medallion is being held by the evil Wrinklewit.

  ISBN 1-4027-0198-5

1.   Maze puzzle—Juvenile literature. [1. Wizards. 2. Maze puzzles. 3. Puzzles.] I. Title

GV1507 .M3 M69 2003

793.73'8—dc21

2002013869

2 4 6 8 10 9 7 5 3 1

Published by Sterling Publishing Co., Inc.

387 Park Avenue South, New York, NY 10016

© 2003 by Roger Moreau

Distributed in Canada by Sterling Publishing

C/o Canadian Manda Group, One Atlantic Avenue, Suite 105

Toronto, Ontario, Canada M6K 3E7

Distributed in Great Britain and Europe by Chris Lloyd at Orca Book

Services, Stanley House, Fleets Lane, Poole BH15 3AJ, England

Distributed in Australia by Capricorn Link (Australia) Pty. Ltd.

P.O. Box 704, Windsor, NSW 2756, Australia

Printed in Hong Kong

Sterling ISBN 1-4027-0198-5

Contents

A Note on the Suggested Use of This Book

As you work your way through the pages of this book, try not to mark them. This will enable you to take this journey over and over again and will also give your friends a chance to take the same journey you took and rescue the wizard.

Special Warning: When the way looks too difficult, avoid the temptation to start at the end and work your way backward. This technique would be a violation of the rules and could result in your losing all your powers.

Cover Maze: Using the appropriate wand, change the rattlesnake into a frog, zap the skunks so they won't stink, and hurry across the bridge before it blows up. Watch out for the dragon's fire and find a clear path to the wizard's castle. This will be good practice for what is ahead.

Introduction

The morning started like any other. Then, suddenly, while you were brushing your teeth, the Ancient Wizard of Wigglewand appeared in the mirror before you. He looked weak and the expression on his face was that of desperation. As he started to speak, you had to catch your breath at the realization that the great Ancient Wizard was about to speak...to you.

"It is with the last ounces of power in me that I am able to appear to you in your mirror. My power is fading fast, so I must be brief. The evil Wrinklewit has stolen my power medallion, taken over Wizardry castle, and cast me into its deepest recesses under lock and key. He has put the village of Wigglewand under his tyranny and closed off all roads to the castle with frightening hazards. It appears as though everyone will live in misery and I will be doomed to eternal confinement. The people of Wigglewand and I need your help to retrieve the power medallion from Wrinklewit and banish him forever. That is why I have selected you.

"If you will help, you must become my apprentice. As my power is fading fast, I will not be able to teach you, so follow these instructions: Go to the Wizard Shopping Mall in the village of Wigglewand. Find the right shop and acquire the magic tools you will find there. In that shop there is a library where I have hidden among the books my 'how-to' wizardry book. There will be a special way that you will be able to identify it over all of the other books. Study this book carefully and learn how to use the tools that you will get in the shop. There will also be an important map that will show the way to Wizardry Castle.

"I have only a little power left. I will finally leave with you this list of magic tools and what they are used for. It is important for you to know that the powers of these tools will be limited because you are only an apprentice and not a fully commissioned wizard. Don't let that discourage you. You must be successful. You are our only hope.

"Here is my list. Copy it down, as it will only stay visible as long as my power lasts."

Tools List

The Wands:

1. Yellow electric wand: Illuminates a dark area. It has limited power for a wizard apprentice.
2. White star wand: Secures the help of snow owls.
3. Fragrance wand: Neutralizes foul smells and makes them smell good. Limited power for a wizard apprentice.
4. Green diamond wand: Changes rattlesnakes into frogs. Limited power for a wizard apprentice.
5. Red fire wand: Freezes and protects you from fire flames. Limited power for a wizard apprentice.
6. Blue star wand: Gives you the power to fly. Limited power for a wizard apprentice.
7. Orange moon-star wand: Freezes spider movement. Limited power for a wizard apprentice.

Magic Red Sand: When cast over an area of tiles, this sand will reveal certain important tiles and eliminate others.

Bow and Arrow: There is nothing magical about the bow and arrow. Practice marksmanship, as you are only given one arrow.

Wizard's Sword: The Ancient Wizard will show you how to use his magic sword, but use it only when called for. It has limited power in the hands of a wizard apprentice.

Prism: The prism will cast the sun's light onto features, revealing important information.

Wizard Shopping Mall

This mall is full of wizard shops, but only one is the true wizard shop. Find your way to the true wizard shop by following the sunstones to the shop's front door. You cannot move diagonally, nor backtrack.

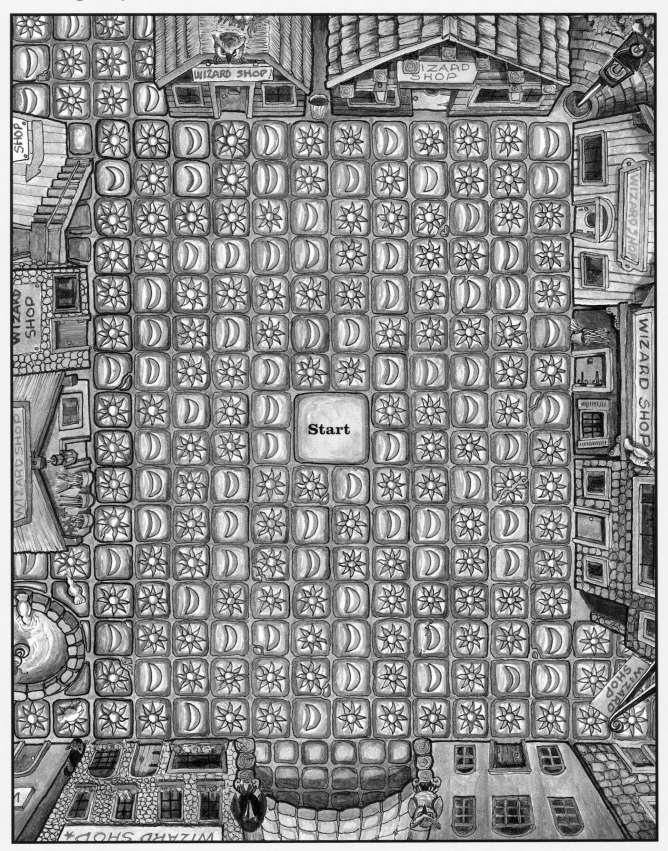

The Wizard's Tools

On the tables in this room are the wizard's tools. You will need all of them on your journey. Pick them up by following the star tiles to each table. Touch each table only once and do not move diagonally or backtrack. Exit on the right into the library.

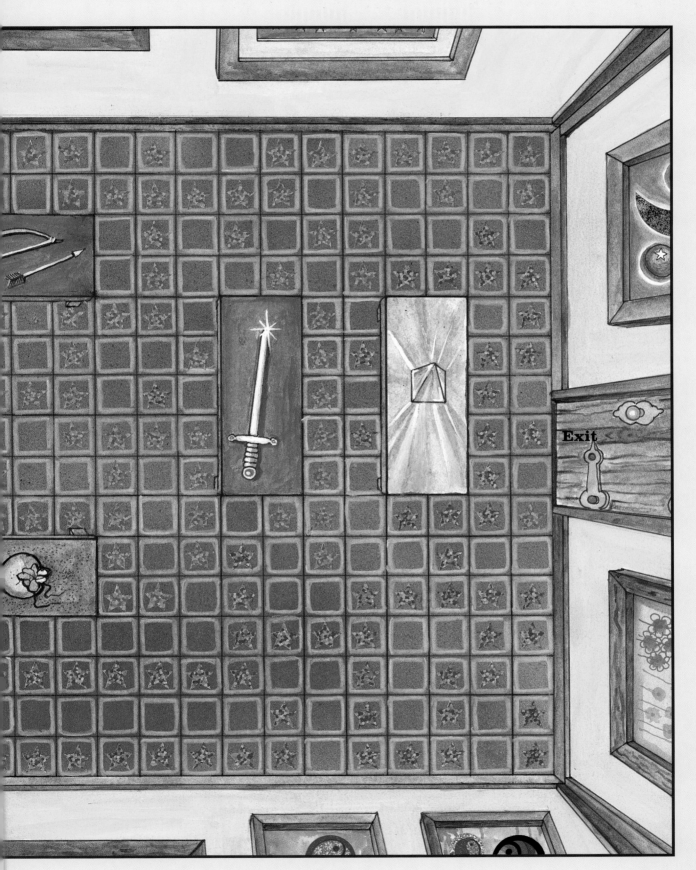

Exit

The Library

Here you must find the wizard's handbook. Find a clear path to the book on the shelf that is surrounded by magic stars.

End

Start

The Wizard's Handbook

This book is securely locked. The magic key can only be used once, so find the correct path to the one keyhole that will open the book. Then turn to the Page of Wands.

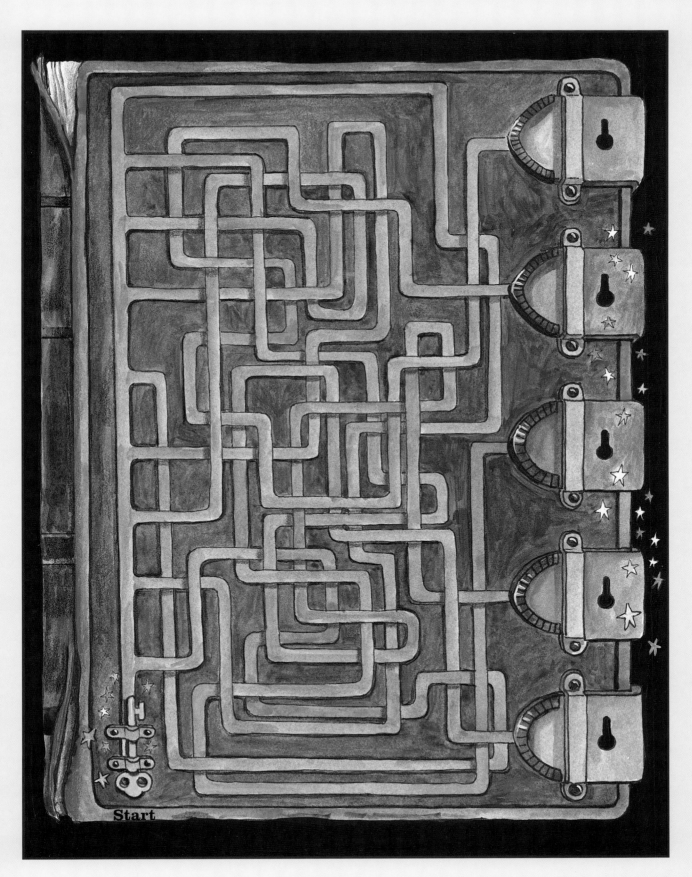

Start

The Page of Wands

You have seven magic wands. Learn their use from this page. The events at the right will require you to use a specific wand when you get to that event on your journey. Place the number of the wand at the left next to the event at the right.

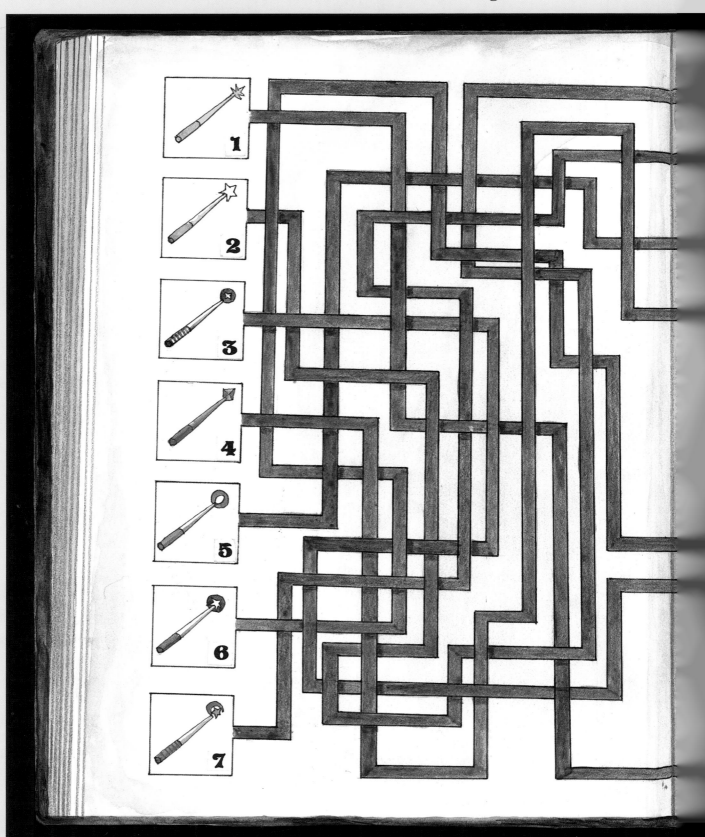

The Map

This map will give you an idea of how to get to the wizard's castle. Find the correct path.

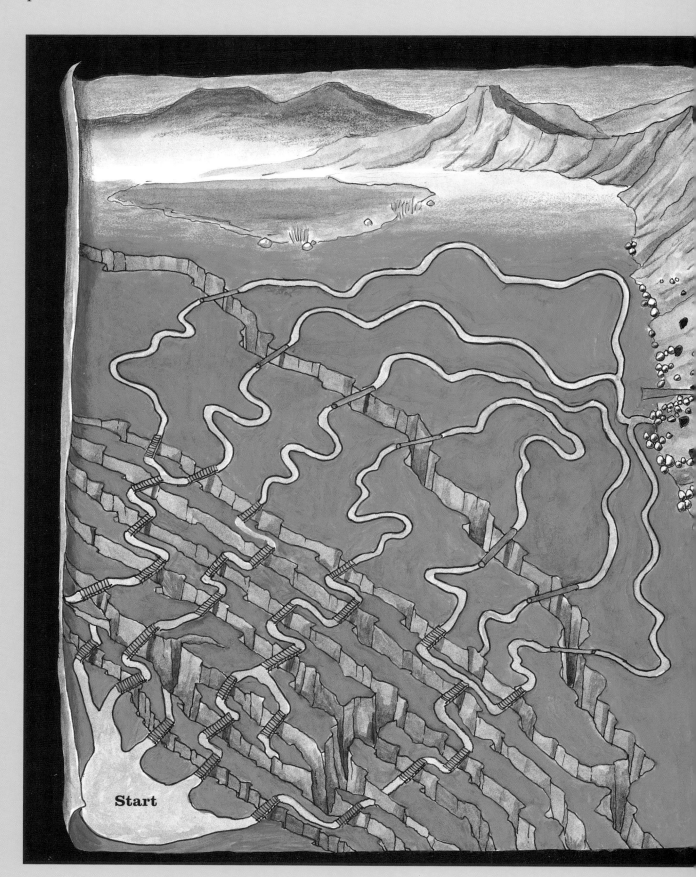

Start

End

15

The Spire

Capture the snow owl at the top of this spire with the correct wand. Halfway up is a ledge. Find your way to the ledge by climbing the connecting rocks and place the number of the correct wand in the square at the foot of the spire. Rest here.

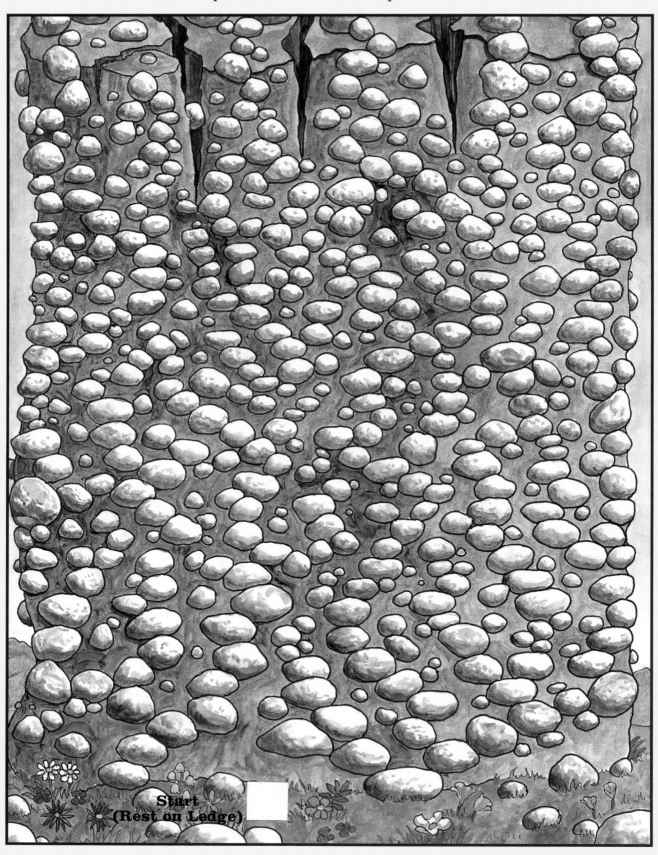

Start
(Rest on Ledge)

The Snow Owl

Continue up the spire to the owl. Wave the correct wand over his head, and he will be your valuable companion throughout your journey.

Start
on Ledge

The Canyon of Bridges

Wrinklewit is trying to stop you by blowing up the bridges. By selecting the correct wand, you will have enough power to fly over two destroyed bridges. Avoid explosions and stay on a path. Put the number of the wand in the box.

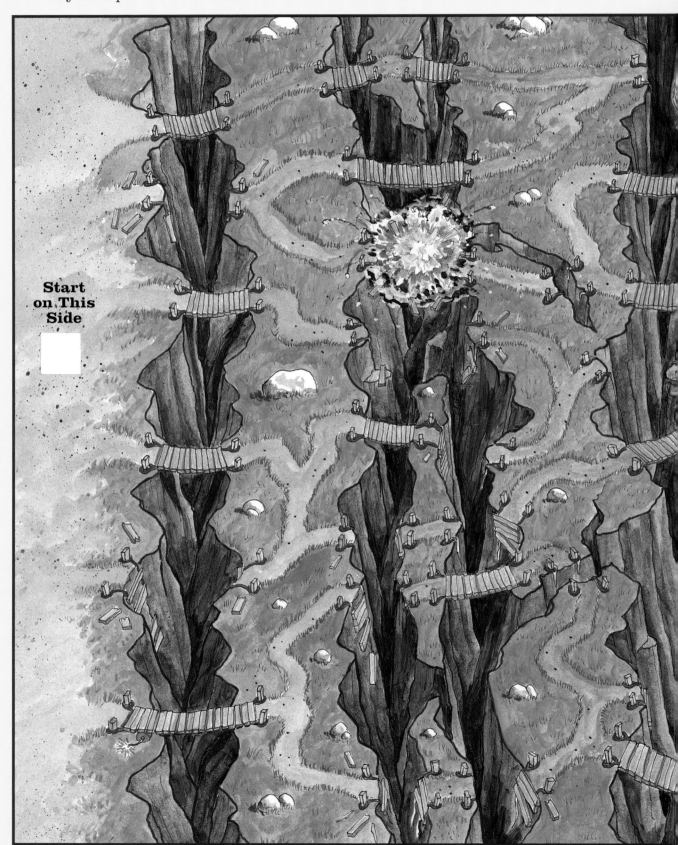

Start on This Side

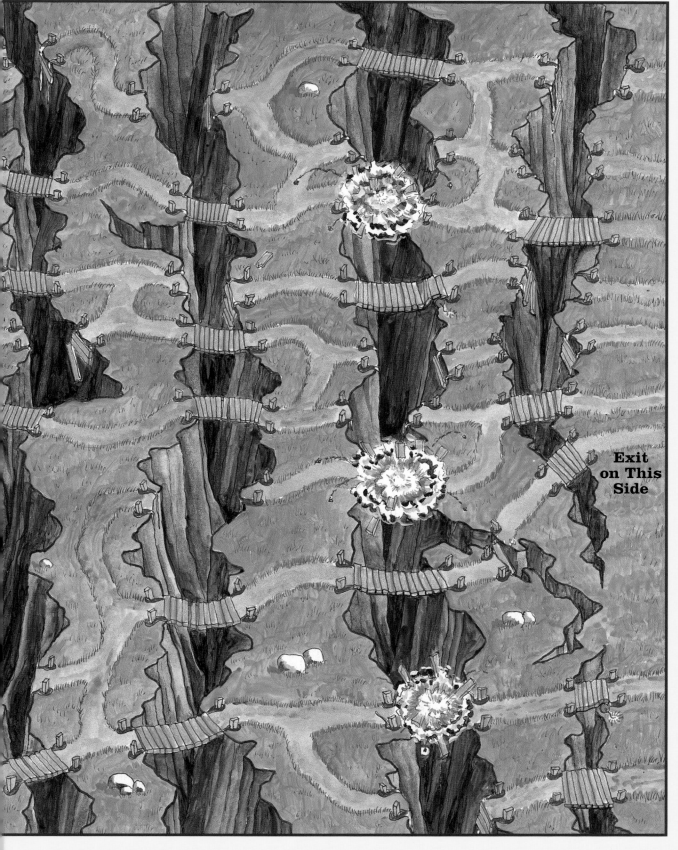

Exit
on This
Side

Rattlesnakes

Wrinklewit is at it again. By using the correct wand, you can change six snakes into frogs. There! See that snake? It's now a frog. Continue on a path. You can change only five more, and don't step over a snake. Put the number of the wand in the box.

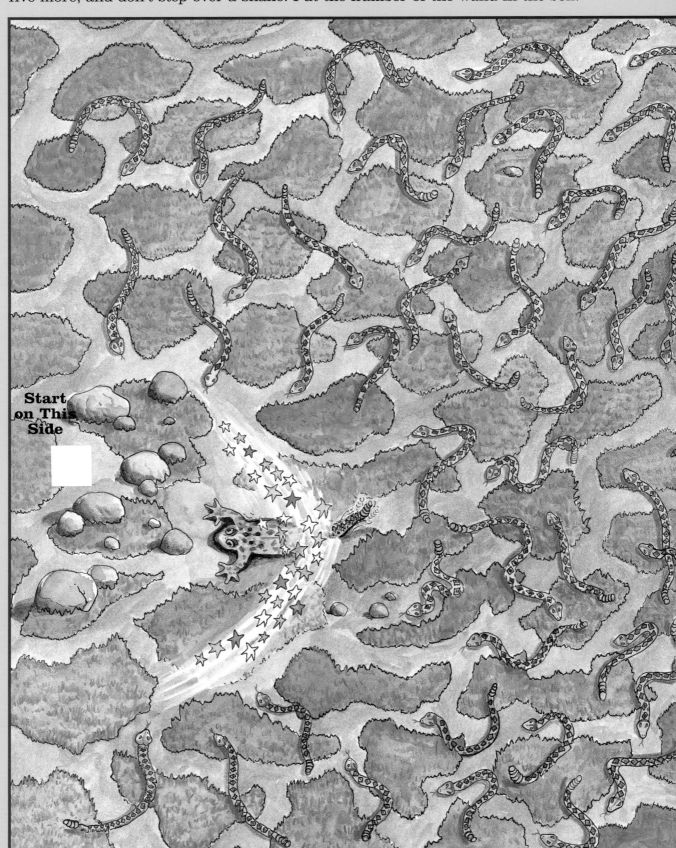

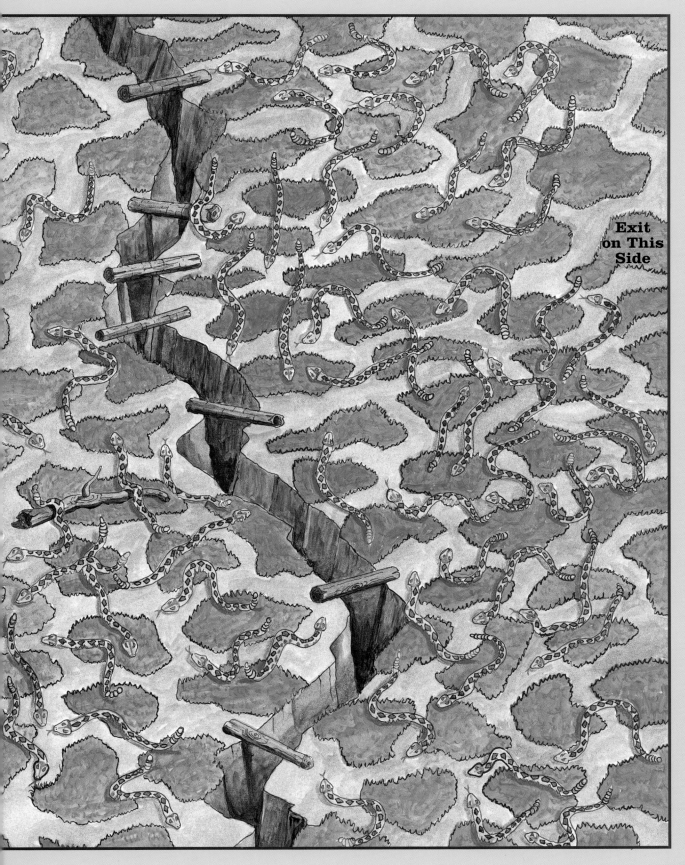

Exit
on This
Side

Skunks

This effort to stop you really stinks. The correct wand has made that one skunk smell like sweet perfume. You can do the same to three more skunks. Find your way to the cliff and put the number of the wand in the box.

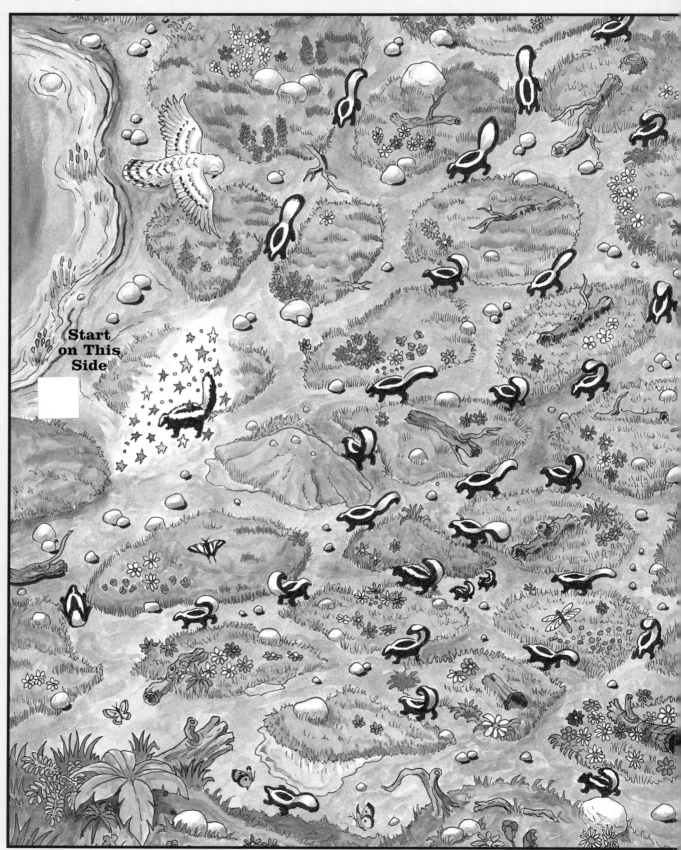

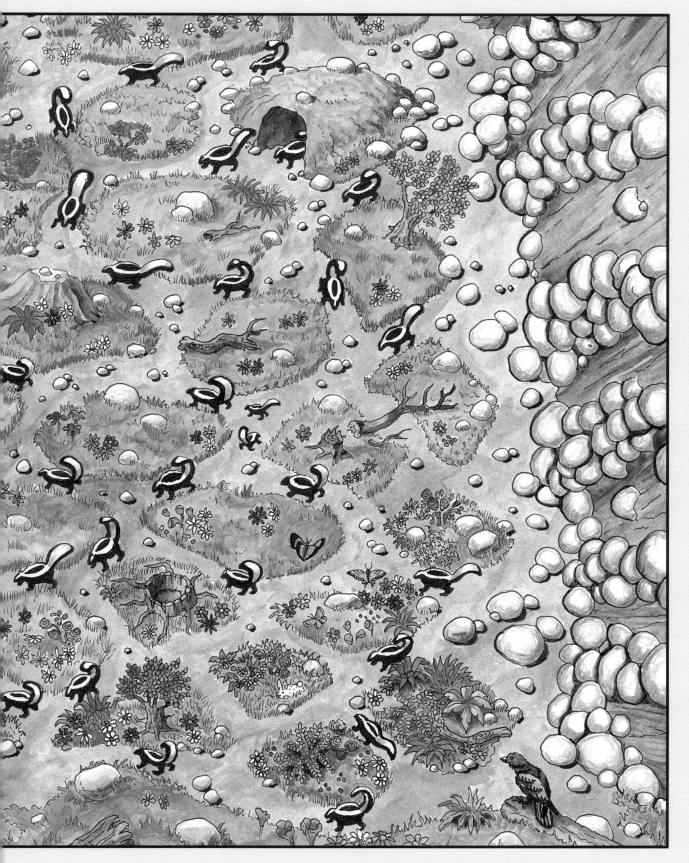

The Cave

Only one cave will lead to the other side of this cliff, but which one? Use the magic prism. Let the sun shine onto it and the correct cave will be revealed. Climb the connecting rocks to its entrance.

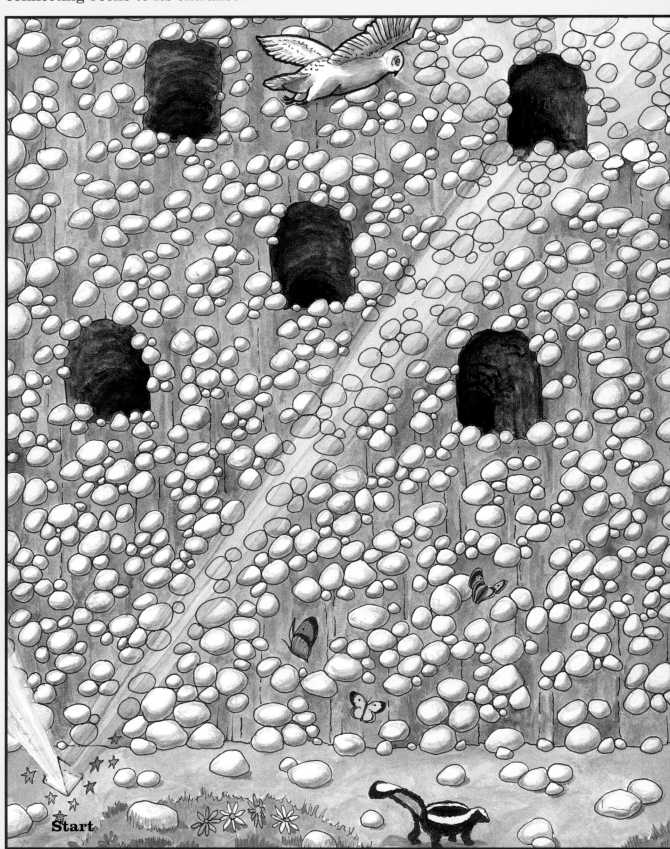

Start

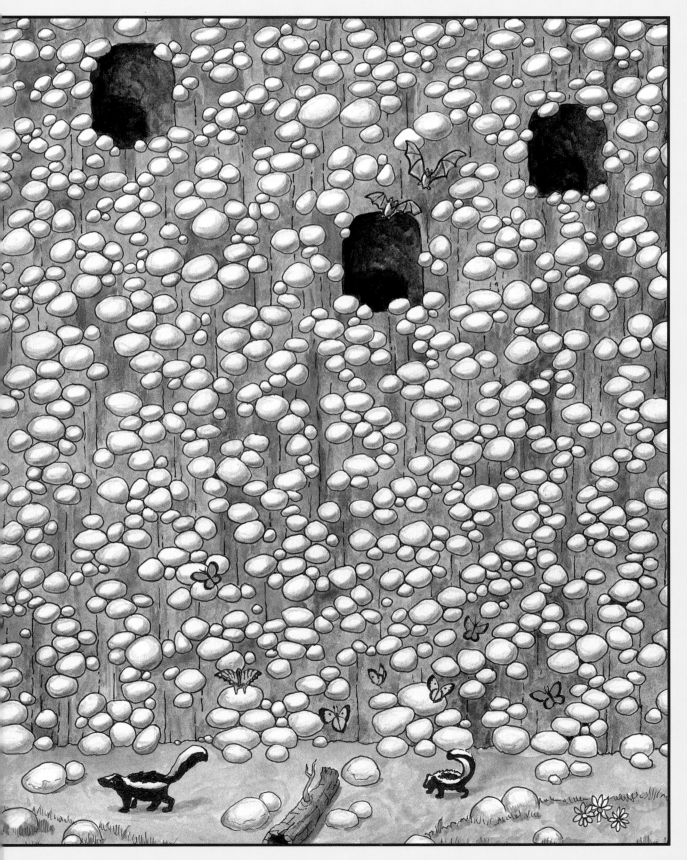

Bats

Bats like the dark, and that's why they live here. The only way you can get through is to use the correct wand and illuminate the cave. Hurry through, because the wand only has enough power to light the cave for two minutes. Find a clear path and put the number of the wand in the box.

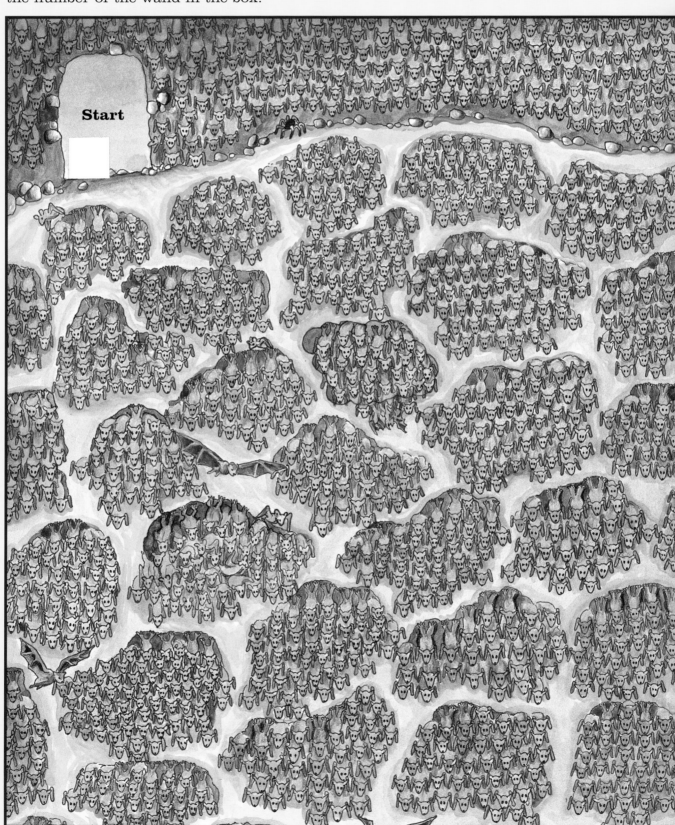

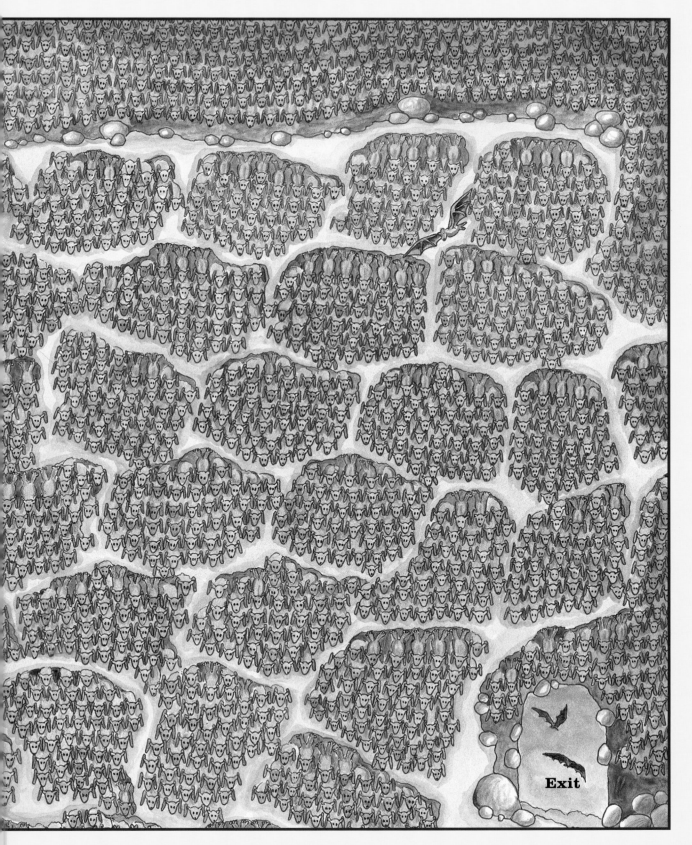

Exit

Baby Dragons

These baby dragons are practicing breathing fire. Find your way by avoiding passing in front of their heads. Let's hope the parents aren't around.

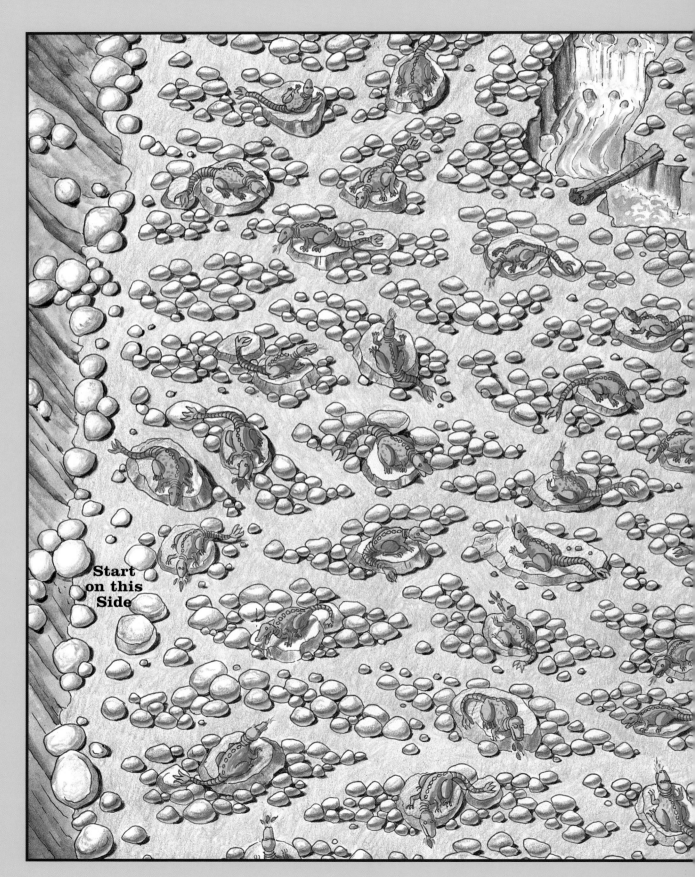

Exit on
this Side

Oh, No! The Parents

These are Wrinklewrit's pets. Use the correct wand and freeze the fire for two minutes. Hurry. Find a clear path past the dragons. Place the number of the wand in the box.

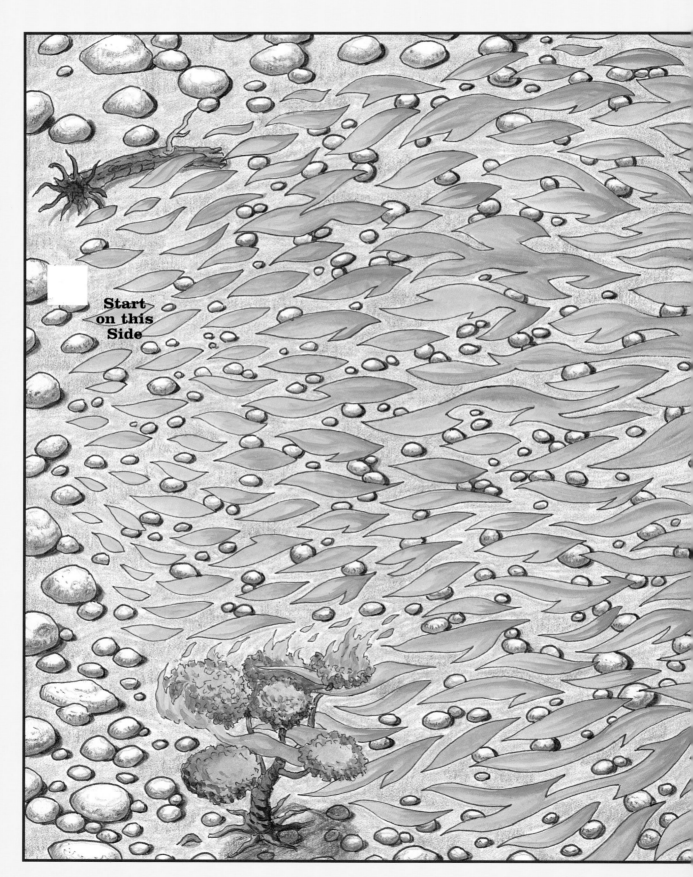

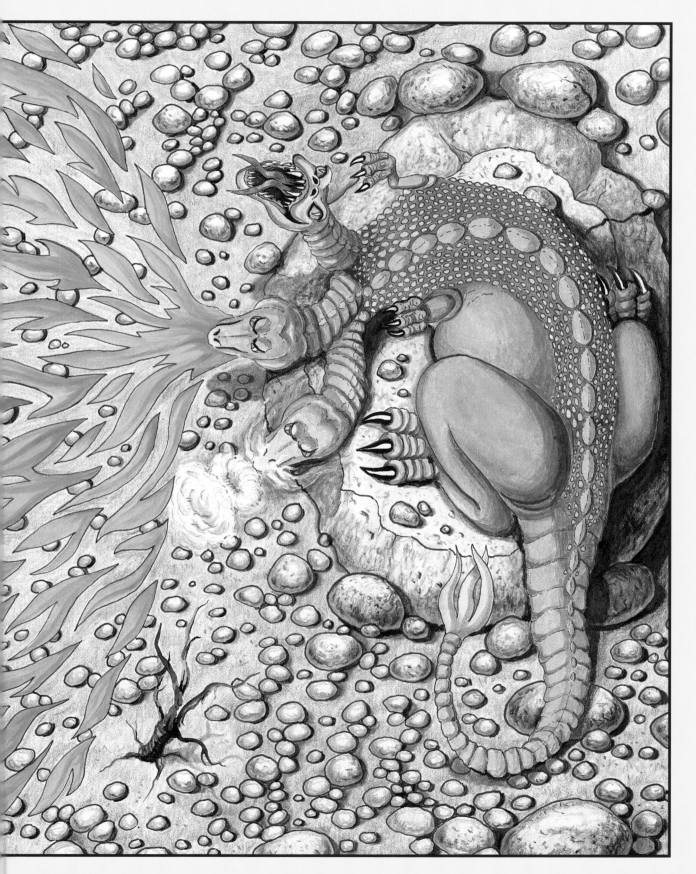

Wizardry Castle

At last you're here. Find a clear path to the castle, but you must line up exactly in front of one of the doors. Next, use the one arrow that you have and shoot it through the hole above the door. The door will open. Enter the castle.

Start Along Any Path

Wrinklewit's Royal Guard

You can't stop these guys. Fight your way to the stairs by using the wizard's magic sword. With it, you can slash your way through only ten swords. It will not work on the spears. Two crossed swords count as two, three count as three, etc.

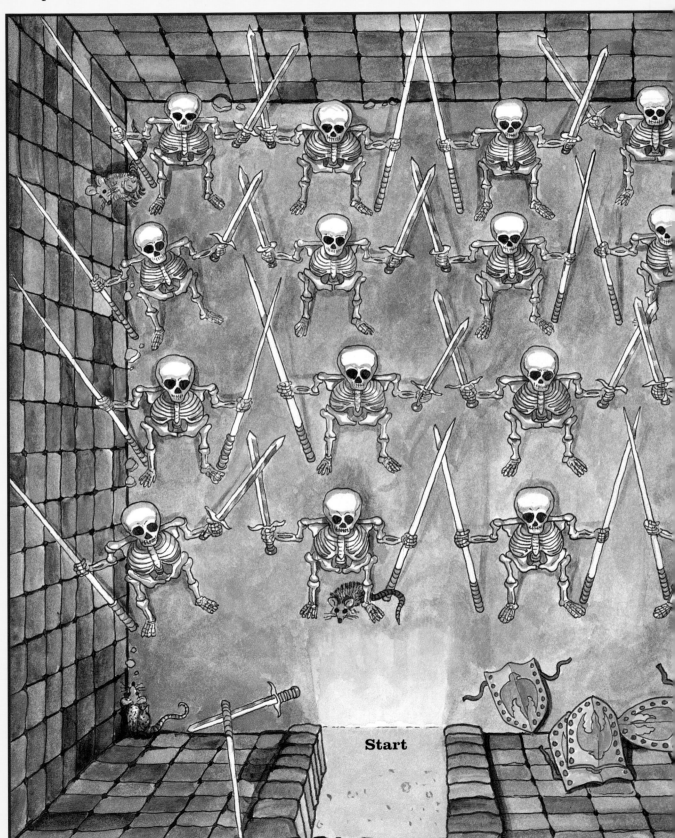

Start

Exit

Spiders

Avoid these spiders. They are aggressive and poisonous, so select the correct wand and paralyze them. You'll have two minutes to find a clear pathway on the web to the doorway in the center of the web. Put the number of the wand in the square.

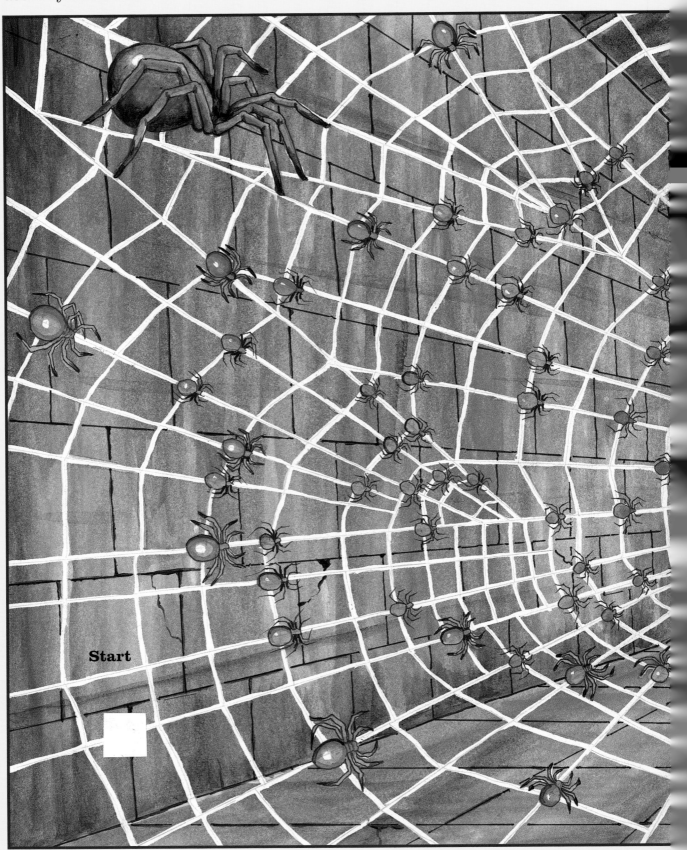

Start

Wrinklewit

Wrinklewit has unleashed bolts of lightning to stop you here. To eliminate his power, obtain the power medallion around his neck. Send the snow owl, as he can fly between the lightning bolts, snatch the medallion, and meet you down those steps on the left.

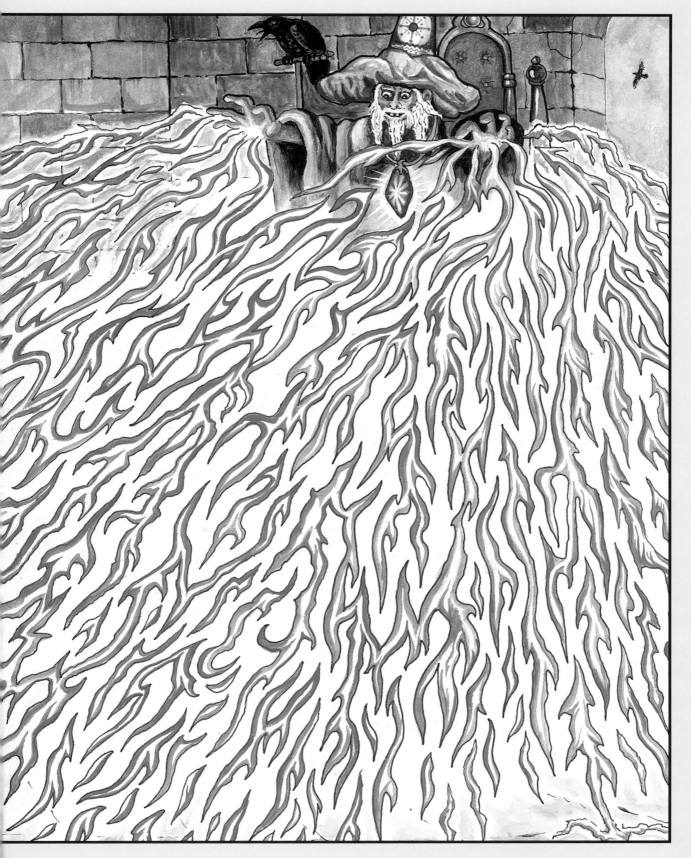

The Mystery Room

One of these doors leads to the dungeon where the wizard is held capture. Cast one bag of the magic red sand over this floor and move on these red tiles to the correct door. You cannot move at a diagonal or backtrack.

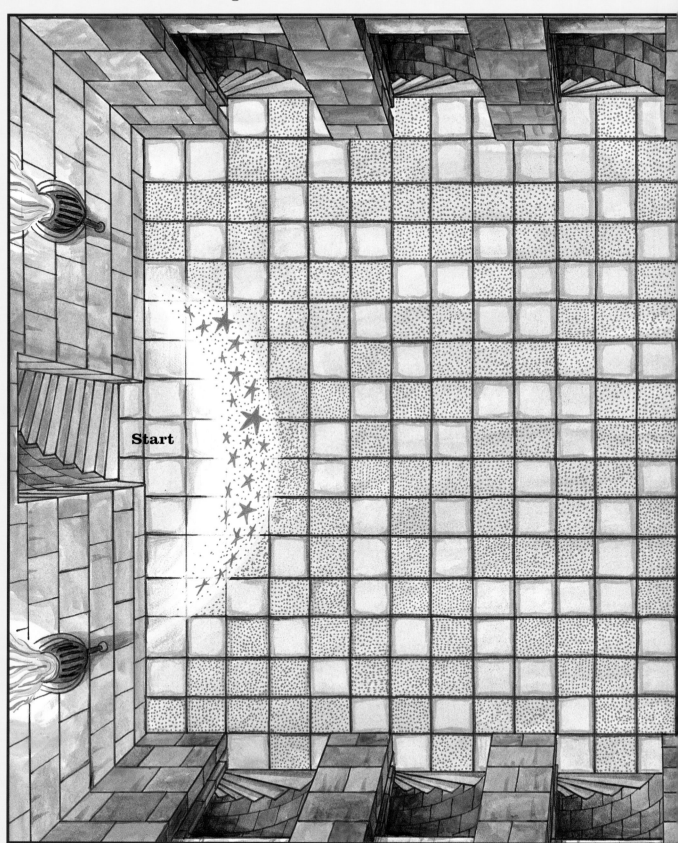

Start

41

The Spiral Stairway

This spiral stairway has collapsed. The only way you can descend is by moving down the connecting protruding blocks.

Stairway Continued

Continue down and exit to the right.

Armor Room

Find your way around the rats to the table on the right side of the room.

Start

Stop
Here

The Pegboard Wall

In order to obtain the key, you must place the thirty pegs into the holes in the wall. You must follow a continuous line of holes until the thirtieth peg ends up in the keyhole. You cannot move diagonally.

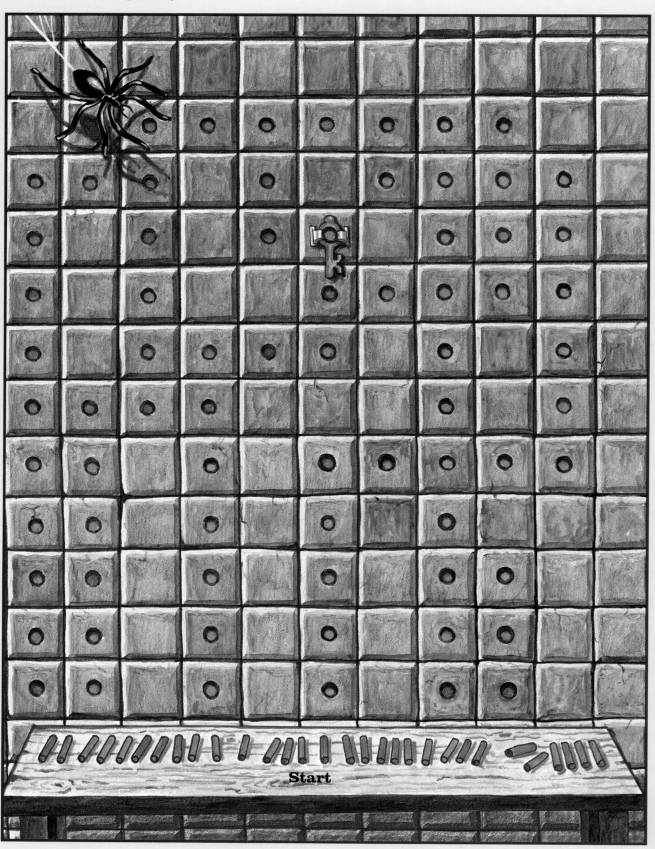

Start

The Cell Door

Find out which keyhole is the correct one by finding a path through the grid to the keyhole. Using the key, open the cell door.

Start

The Wizard

There he is, and he's well locked up. To find out the combination to unlock the wizard's cell, you must cast your last bag of magic red sand over the floor. Follow the red tiles

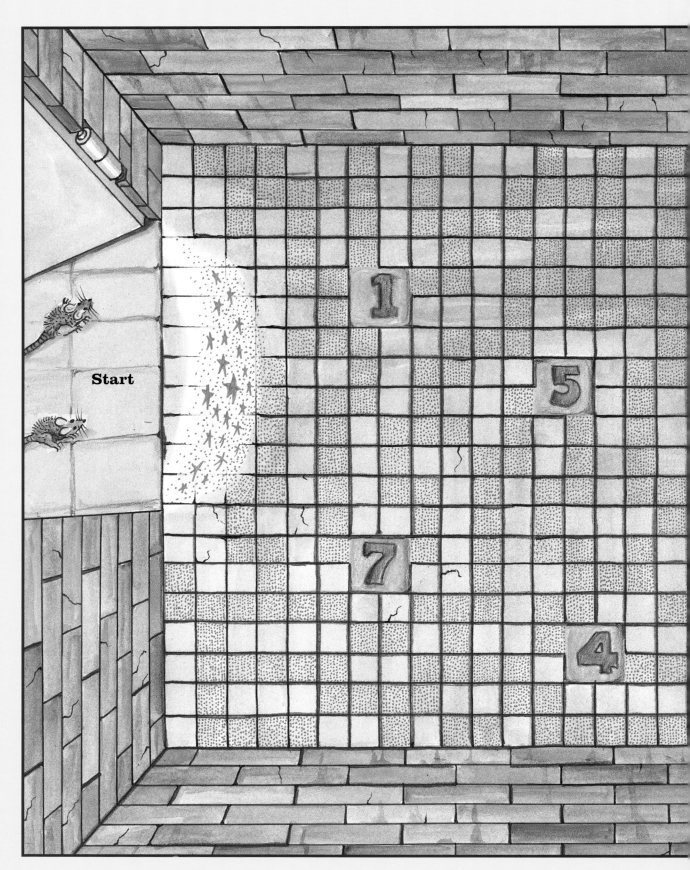

to the numbers and place each number on the lock, beginning at the top with the first number you come to. The problem is you can only visit each number once, and cannot move diagonally or backtrack.

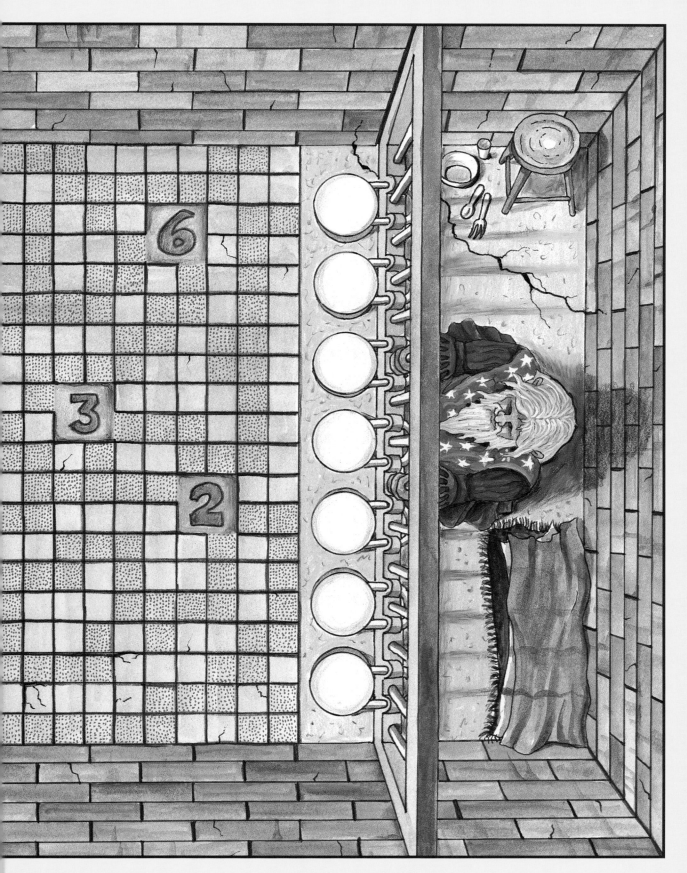

Celebration Time

Wigglewand has been liberated, the Ancient Wizard's free and his power restored. It's time to celebrate, and you are the honored guest. Make your way to the platform

Start

where the wizard and snow owl are by finding a path around the people. You can step on rocks, grass, everything. Just avoid bumping into people.

Congratulations!

For a long time, the village of Wigglewand had been terrorized and held hostage by the evil Wrinklewit when he gained power by capturing the power medallion from the Ancient Wizard. Thanks to you, the villagers' freedoms and the wizard's powers have been restored. As a young wizard apprentice, you took the time to acquire the tools, study the ways, and practice the magic to achieve what was needed to be done—banish Wrinklewit, restore the villagers' freedoms, and restore the Ancient Wizard to his righteous rule. The people of Wigglewand thank you, and the Ancient Wizard thanks you. You had to face all of the obstacles that Wrinklewit threw at you, and you won. What you have learned will be of great value. Who knows, perhaps one day you might succeed the Ancient Wizard himself.

Solutions to all of the mazes are on the following pages.

Cover Maze/Wizard Shopping Mall

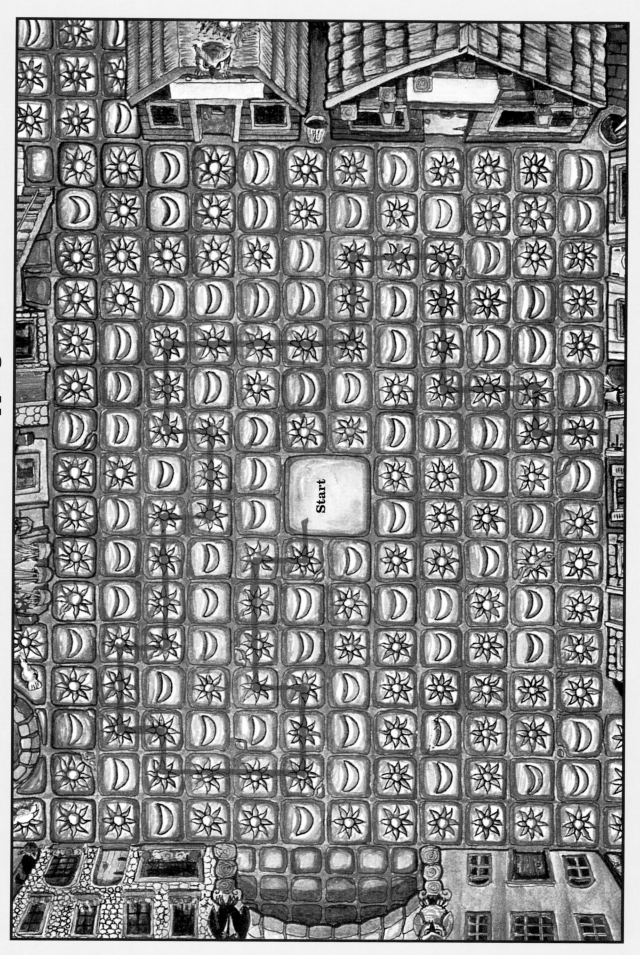

Start

The Wizard's Tools

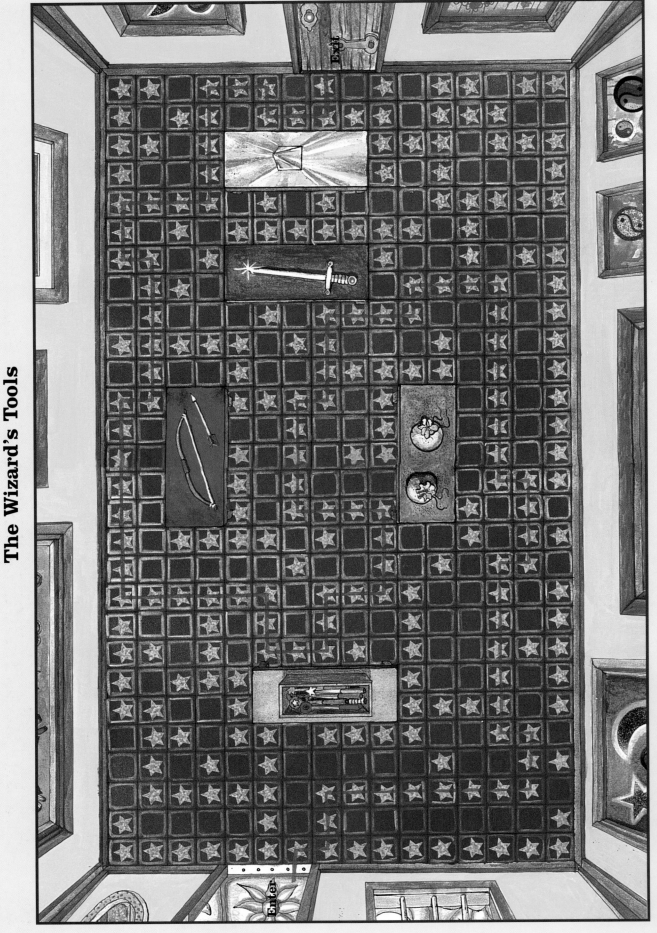

The Library

End

Start

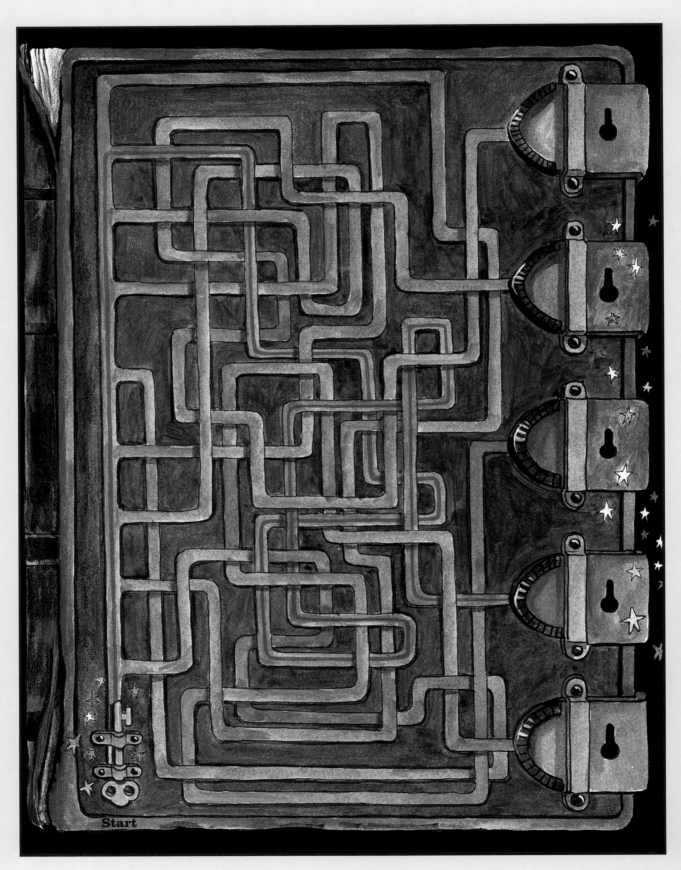

Start

The Page of Wands

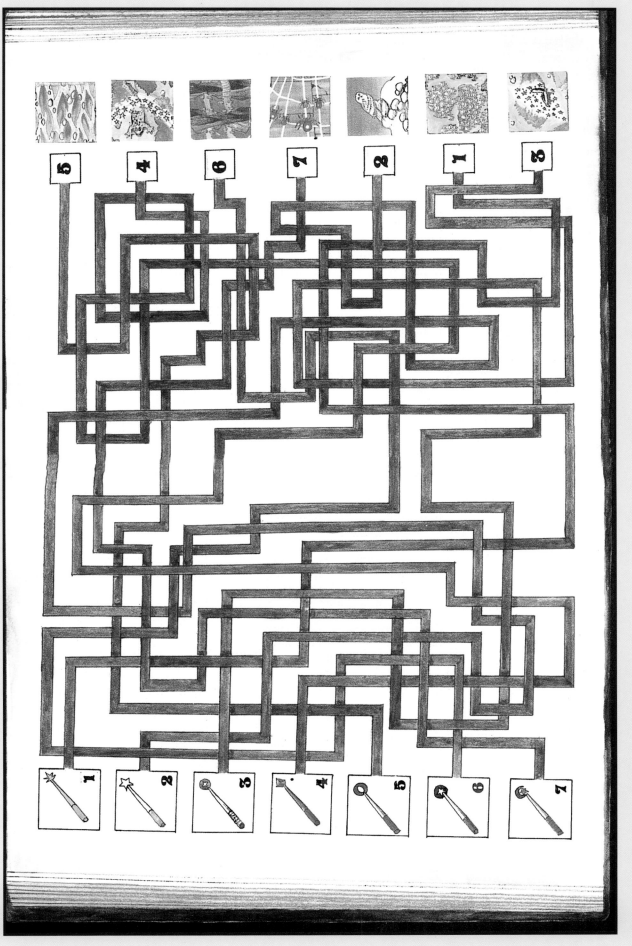

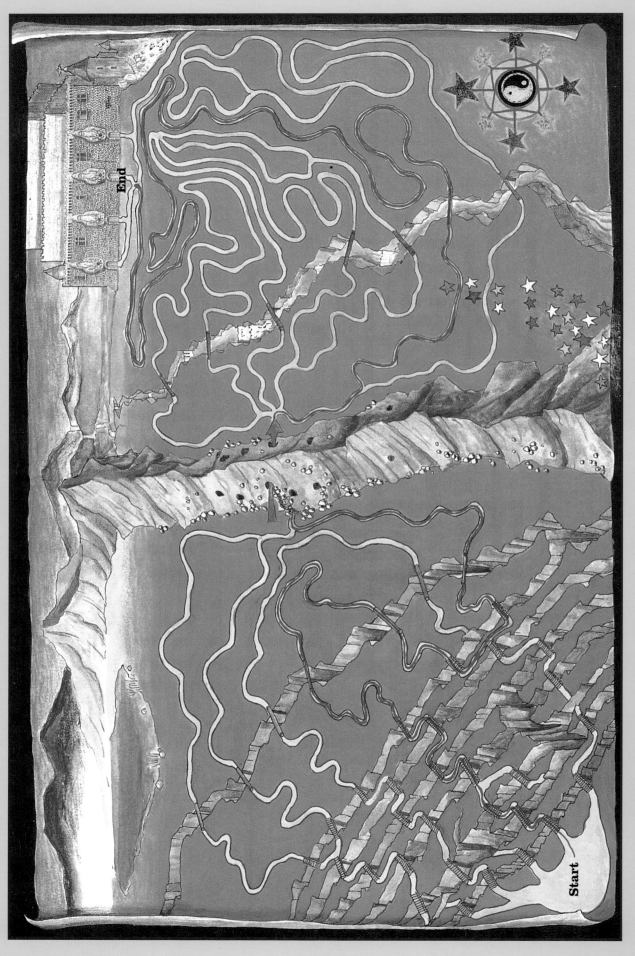

The Map

The Spire

Start
(Rest on Ledge)

2

The Snow Owl

Start
on Ledge

The Canyon of Bridges

Rattlesnakes

Exit on This Side

Start on This Side

4

Skunks

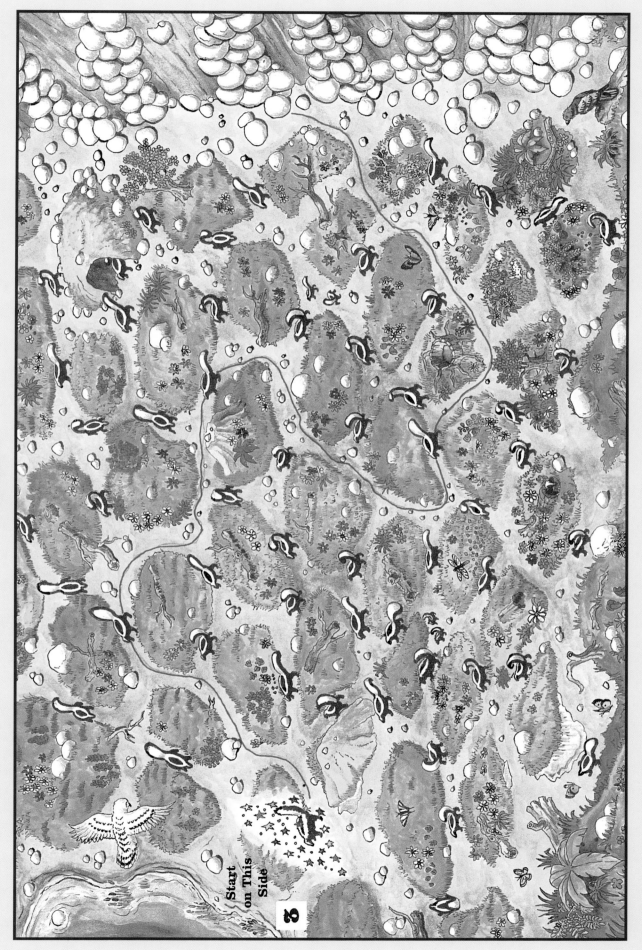

Start on This Side

3

The Cave

Start

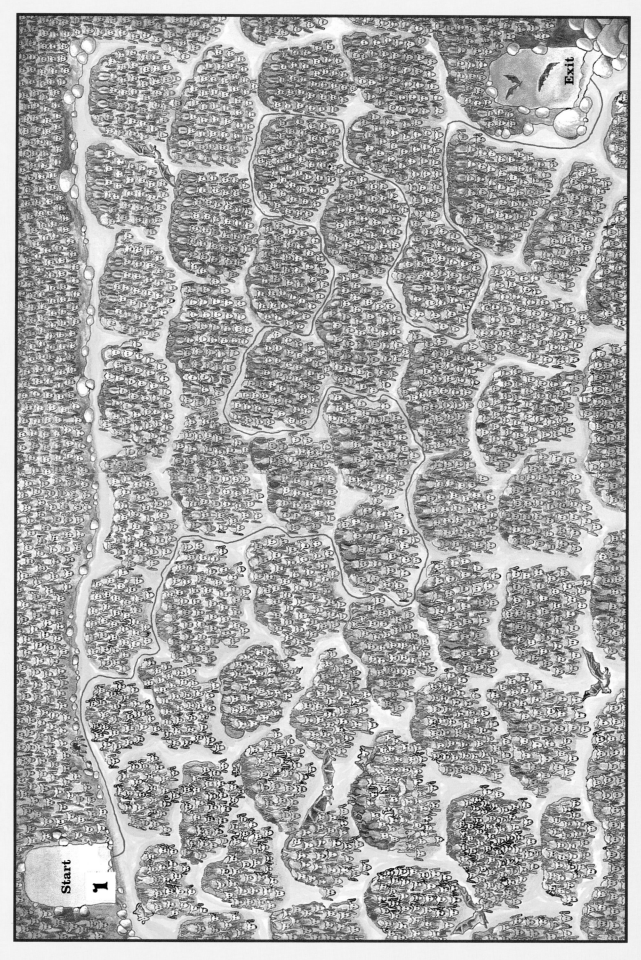

Bats

Start

1

Exit

Baby Dragons

Exit on
this Side

Start on
this Side

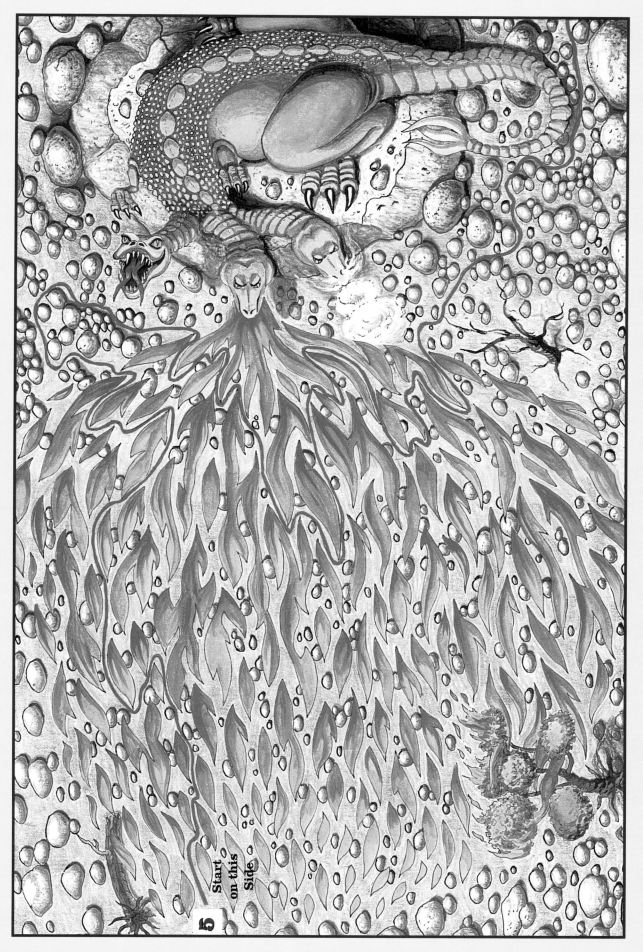

5

Start
on this
Side

Wizardry Castle

Start Along Any Path

Wrinklewit's Royal Guard

Spiders

Start

70

Wrinklewit

Start

End

The Mystery Room

Start

The Spiral Stairway

Start

Exit

Armor Room

Stop Here

Start

The Pegboard Wall

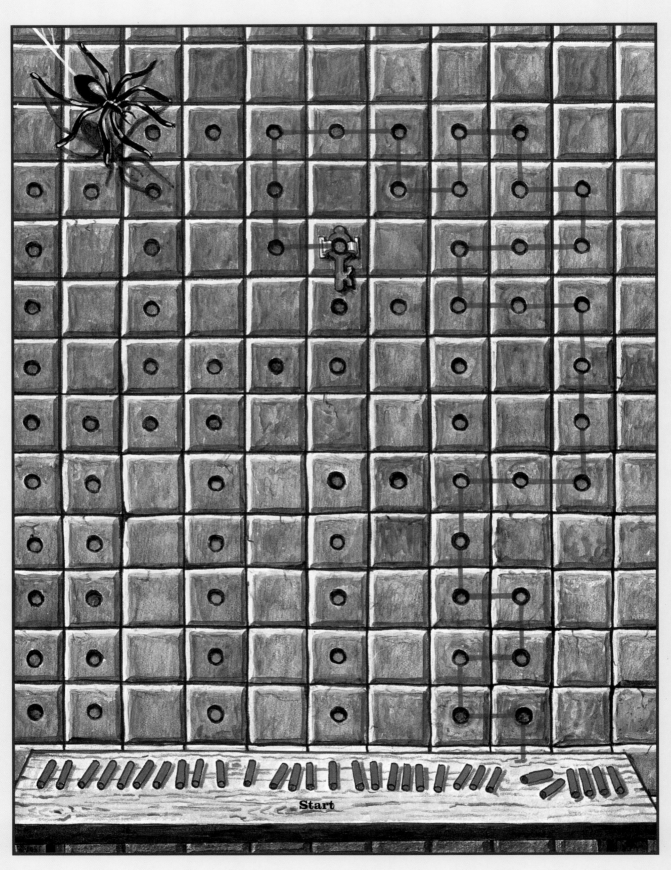

Start

The Cell Door

Start

The Wizard

Start

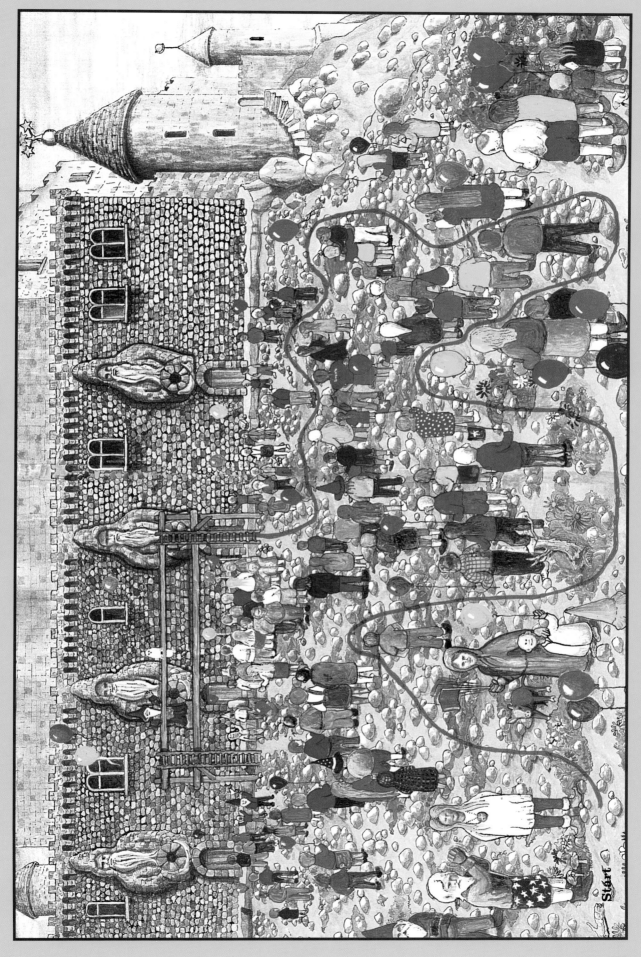

Index

Page numbers in **bold** refer to answer mazes.